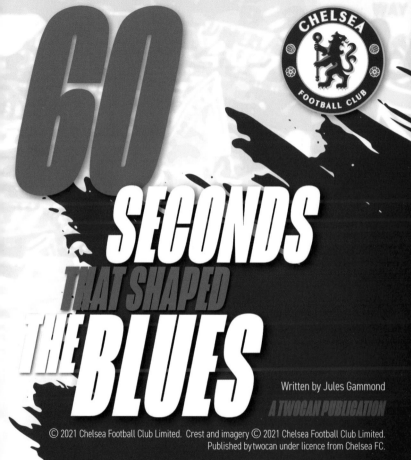

60

SECONDS

THAT SHAPED

THE BLUES

Written by Jules Gammond

A TWOCAN PUBLICATION

ISBN: 978-1-914588-49-5

PICTURE CREDITS:
Action Images, Alamy, Getty Images.

60 Seconds that Shaped the Blues

Selecting 60 memorable moments from the decorated history of Chelsea Football Club has been a difficult, but enjoyable task as there have been so many to choose from, particularly in the last couple of decades under the ownership of Roman Abramovich.

Indeed, since 2003 when he bought the club, the Blues have won two Champions Leagues, five Premierships, five FA Cups, three League Cups and two Europa Leagues. Not that they were entirely unsuccessful before, as the Stamford Bridge trophy cabinet already included a first league title, three more FA Cups and two Cup Winners' Cups.

Chelsea FC Women have been no less prolific, winning five league titles, two FA Cups and two League Cups. But this book is not exclusively about triumphs, it recalls those important milestones in Chelsea Football Club's life story, the year it was founded, the chairmen and managers who made an indelible mark over the years, the record scores and classic games, the goalscorers and legends, that have each contributed to the rich tapestry that is Chelsea FC.

Having been a supporter for more than 50 years, I have been privileged to have witnessed many of the highs and lows first hand, including that soggy night in Moscow when, but for a slip by captain John Terry in the penalty shoot-out, we would have won three Champions League trophies by now. And while our fans sing about being 'carefree' it is because we care so deeply that this collection of magical moments will bring a tear to the eye and lump to the throat of all true Blues 'wherever you may be'.

Come On You Blues!

Jules Gammond

GUS MEARS

Chelsea Football Club was founded in the Rising Sun Public House, now the Butcher's Hook, in the Fulham Road on 10 March 1905.

The Birth Of The Blues

#1

Founding father Gus Mears had acquired the Stamford Bridge athletics stadium in 1904 with the aim of turning it into a football ground.

A munificent free-spirit, he offered to lease it to Fulham Football Club, but was turned down and decided to form his own club. The founding meeting was held in an upstairs room of a pub opposite the main entrance to Stamford Bridge - a popular local venue that often hosted inquests as well as freemasons meetings.

The club did not want to use the name Fulham - that club already played in the borough - so adopted the name of the adjacent borough, Chelsea, after considering such names as Kensington FC, Stamford Bridge FC and London FC. Chelsea Football & Athletic Club was registered at Companies House on 20 April 1905 with a capital of £5,000 from 3,505 allotted shares.

Unlike the industrial moguls who had founded midland and northern clubs, the driving forces behind Chelsea were entrepreneurs, publicans and a broader band of influential and well-to-do supporters. The first president was Lord Cadogan, the largest landowner in the area whose Eton blue racing colours were worn for the first two seasons, before the club switched to royal blue, the official club colour that has become synonymous with Chelsea Football Club for more than a century.

FIXTURE: League Division Two

DATE: 2 September 1905

SCORE: Stockport County 1
Chelsea 0

VENUE: Edgeley Park

ATTENDANCE: 7,000

Chelsea's First Ever Fixture

The trip to Cheshire to face Lancashire Combination champions Stockport County produced a tight affair against a side who already had Division Two experience.

JIMMY WINDRIDGE

Chelsea's 22-stone goalkeeper, William 'Fatty' Foulke, saved a second-half penalty from Ashton Schofield only for George Dodd to tap in the rebound with half an hour to play and give the hosts the two points.

This was followed by another away match at Blackpool, from which Chelsea gained their first two points of the season thanks to a late winner from player-manager Jacky Robertson, thus becoming Chelsea's first-ever league goalscorer.

Chelsea played their first home league match at Stamford Bridge against newly-promoted Hull City on 11 September, with the Blues storming to a 5-1 win. Jimmy Windridge hit the club's first hat-trick during the game while Foulke saved another penalty, his second in three matches.

WILLIAM 'FATTY' FOULKE WITH
BOB MACKIE AND DAVIE COPELAND

At the end of their first season,
Chelsea, by now already known as the Pensioners,
finished third in the division, missing out on promotion
after failing to win five matches in a row at the
end of the campaign.

CHELSEA

Royal Blue Shirts and White Knickers

1
MOLYNEUX
Goal

2
BETTRIDGE
Right Back

3
HARROW
Left Back

4
TAYLOR
Right Half

5
LOGAN
Centre Half

6
WALKER
Left Half

7
FORD
Outside Right

8
HALSE
Inside Right

9
THOMSON
Centre

10
CROAL
Inside Left

11
M'N
Outside

Referee:
Mr. H. H. TAYLOR

KICK-OFF. 3-30.

14
KITCHEN

15
FAZACKERLEY

16
SIMMON
Outside Rig

URGESS
Right Half

OK

*Chelsea reached the FA Cup final
for the first time in April 1915. Pitted against
Sheffield United, it was the last cup final to be staged
before competitive football was suspended during WWI.*

FIXTURE: FA Cup final

DATE: 24 April 1915

SCORE: Sheffield United 3
Chelsea 0

VENUE: Old Trafford

ATTENDANCE: 49,557

#3

Chelsea's First FA Cup Final

For a match known as the Khaki Cup final, due to the large number of uniformed soldiers in attendance, Sheffield United were firm favourites as Chelsea were languishing in the relegation zone.

The Blues had however, beaten several strong sides to get to the final, including Arsenal, Manchester City, Newcastle United and Everton in the semi-final. One of the club's star players, Vivian Woodward, was serving in the British Army and had been given leave to play in the final, but sportingly insisted that Bob Thomson, the club's leading goalscorer that season, should play as he had helped the team reach the final.

The match was a dull, one-sided affair with Sheffield United's pacy players outclassing Chelsea and scoring through Simmons, Fazackerley and Kitchen. A thick fog descended over the pitch in the second half, preventing spectators from seeing much of the action, with The Times commenting that they were not missing much.

More FA Cup joy was to come for Chelsea fans over the years, with the Blues going on to appear in 15 finals, winning eight of them.

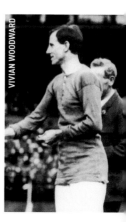

VIVIAN WOODWARD

FIXTURE:	League Division One
DATE:	12 October 1935
SCORE:	Chelsea 1
	Arsenal 1
VENUE:	Stamford Bridge
ATTENDANCE:	82,905

#4

Record Crowd
For Gunners Visit

An amazing 82,905 fans crammed into Stamford Bridge to see the Blues take on defending champions Arsenal, who were trying to win their third consecutive title.

JOE BAMBRICK V BOLTON, APRIL 1937

At the time, it was the largest-ever attendance in Football League history, but has subsequently been surpassed by Tottenham Hotspur's attendance of 83,222 against Arsenal at Wembley Stadium in 2018.

The game lived up to its billing as the 'greatest-ever match' with the Gunners hanging on for a hard-earned draw after Jack Crayton's late goal for the Gunners cancelled out Joe Bambrick's second-half strike for Chelsea.

The Chelsea vs Arsenal fixture is London's longest-running top-flight rivalry, which began with a 2-1 Chelsea victory at Stamford Bridge in November 1907.

*The Blues' thumping
6-0 triumph in March 2014 remains the largest
victory between the two London giants, while Didier
Drogba is the fixture's top scorer with 13 goals.*

*The final between
Chelsea and Millwall in April 1945 was the
first club match to be attended by Princess Elizabeth,
the future Queen Elizabeth II.*

FIXTURE: Football League South Cup final

DATE: 7 April 1945

SCORE: Chelsea 2
Millwall 0

VENUE: Wembley

ATTENDANCE: 90,000

Royals Watch Wembley Win

Accompanying her father, King George VI, who was introduced to the teams before kick-off, the Princess watched Chelsea beat Millwall 2-0 in the Wembley final.

With the war in Europe coming to an end, the number of spectators allowed to attend games was relaxed and 90,000 fans filled Wembley Stadium in a celebratory mood.

The tournament, which was set up to fill the hole left by the cancellation of the traditional FA Cup during the war, was split into northern and southern halves. The winners of each section competed in a Play-Off at Stamford Bridge to decide the victor. After beating Millwall in the South Cup final, Chelsea played Bolton Wanderers, who had beaten Manchester United over two legs, at the Bridge on 2 June 1945.

While Chelsea narrowly lost the overall final to Bolton, they had already made history by being in the first final ever watched by the future queen, while Blues centre-half 'Gentleman John' Harris became the first Chelsea captain to lift a trophy at Wembley, receiving the Football League South Cup from King George VI.

JOE PAYNE CHALLENGES
KEEPER SAM BARTRAM

FIXTURE:	Friendly
DATE:	13 November 1945
SCORE:	Chelsea 3 Dynamo Moscow 3
VENUE:	Stamford Bridge
ATTENDANCE:	74,496

#6

First Russian Team Visit after WWII

With Britain beginning a slow return to normality after the Second World War, the football authorities announced a morale booster: the Soviet Union's leading club, Dynamo Moscow, would play a series of friendlies against top British sides.

TOMMY LAWTON AND MOSCOW
GOALKEEPER ALEXEI KHOMICH

Chelsea were honoured with the first match of the tour against our allies' best football team. Curiosity about the mystery opponents and years without regular football prompted huge interest, and an enormous crowd turned up at the Bridge - the 'unofficial' attendance was estimated to be in the region of 100,000 to 120,000 fans.

To add further spice to the occasion, Chelsea featured iconic England centre-forward Tommy Lawton, who they had signed a week earlier from Everton for a record fee of £11,500. Lawton headed the Blues' third goal, following strikes by Reg Williams and Len Goulden, but the visitors hit back and scored three times in the final 20 minutes to earn an honourable draw.

Dynamo's leveller was reputedly five yards offside, although the referee later told Lawton that he had made the decision to allow it for 'diplomatic reasons'.

REG WILLIAMS CHALLENGES DYNAMO MOSCOW'S IVAN STANKEVICH
DEFLECTING THE BALL INTO THE NET FOR CHELSEA'S SECOND GOAL

*After the match,
praise was heaped on the celebrated players,
with the game being described as one of the best
football matches ever seen on English soil.*

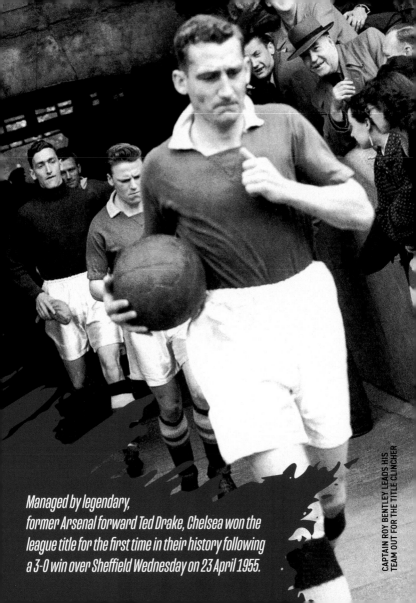

Managed by legendary, former Arsenal forward Ted Drake, Chelsea won the league title for the first time in their history following a 3-0 win over Sheffield Wednesday on 23 April 1955.

CAPTAIN ROY BENTLEY LEADS HIS TEAM OUT FOR THE TITLE CLINCHER

FIXTURE:	League Division One
DATE:	23 April 1955
SCORE:	Chelsea 3 Sheffield Wednesday 0
VENUE:	Stamford Bridge
ATTENDANCE:	51,421

League Champions
For The First Time

Finally the wait was over. After five decades of hope and expectation, the Blues were crowned Football League champions in the 50th year since their foundation.

Eric 'Rabbit' Parsons scored twice while a Peter Sillett penalty made it 3-0, and as the crowd poured onto the pitch at the end of the game, a microphone was hastily rigged up on the upper tier of the East Stand for an emotional Drake, flanked by his players, to tell the fans: "This is the happiest moment of my life. I congratulate all the boys and every one of my staff - office, training and playing. Right throughout, they are one and all Chelsea!"

The players, captained by top scorer Roy Bentley, were offered a title-winning bonus of £20 or a tailored suit, and many chose the latter, knowing they had written themselves into Chelsea folklore.

When Drake was appointed manager in June 1952, he had predicted it would take three years to turn the underperforming Chelsea into champions of England. Like a certain 'Special One' some 50 years later, he had even predicted the season.

FANS INVADE THE PITCH AT THE FINAL WHISTLE

FIXTURE:	Friendly
DATE:	19 March 1957
SCORE:	Chelsea 2
	Sparta Prague 0
VENUE:	Stamford Bridge
ATTENDANCE:	30,708

#8

First Match Under Floodlights

Stamford Bridge's new floodlights had been tested during a youth team fixture, but they were given their official baptism a few days later against Sparta Prague.

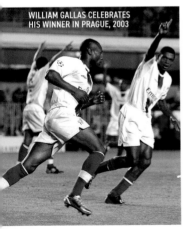

WILLIAM GALLAS CELEBRATES
HIS WINNER IN PRAGUE, 2003

Chelsea were relative latecomers to the post-war floodlight revolution, but had played under electric lights some 30 years previously - on 28 June 1929 in Rio de Janeiro, Brazil against a combined Carioca XI.

More than 30,000 fans turned up at the Bridge to see a strong first team including Matthews, Whittaker, Sillett, Mortimore, Dicks, Saunders, Brabrook, McNichol, Allen, Gibbs and Laverick take on the historic European side. The match kicked off at 7.45pm and was settled with goals from Allen and Gibbs.

The first competitive match between the sides did not come until the 2003/04 UEFA Champions League group stage, when a 1-0 away win for the Blues was followed by a 0-0 home draw as Chelsea went top of the group.

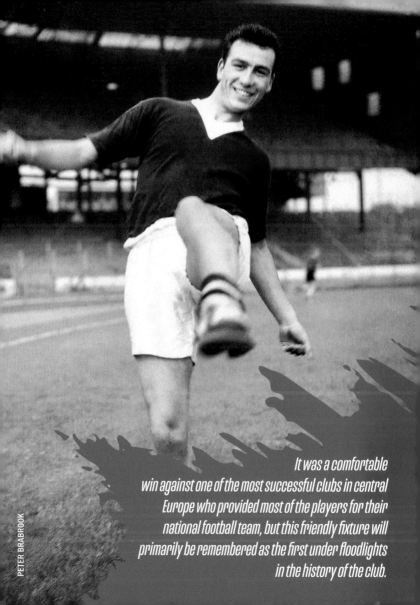

PETER BRABROOK

It was a comfortable win against one of the most successful clubs in central Europe who provided most of the players for their national football team, but this friendly fixture will primarily be remembered as the first under floodlights in the history of the club.

*The infamous
'Battle of the Bridge' took place on
a September evening in 1965 when Chelsea hosted
a volatile AS Roma in a toxic European tie.*

FIXTURE: Fairs Cup

DATE: 22 September 1965

SCORE: Chelsea 4
AS Roma 1

VENUE: Stamford Bridge

ATTENDANCE: 32,753

#9

Battle Of The Bridge

The Italian visitors' crude tackling and unsportsmanlike behaviour infuriated full-back Eddie McCreadie so much, that he was sent off for a retaliatory punch.

But it did not affect the result as a rare Terry Venables hat-trick and a George Graham strike made the visit to Rome something of a formality.

The Italian fans were in feisty form, throwing missiles at the visiting players and attacking the coach on its return to the airport. A goalless draw was good enough to take the Blues through and their spectacular run continued, beating the likes of AC Milan (the tie decided on the toss of a coin after the scores were level) and Munich 1860, before a semi-final meeting with Barcelona. The Blues took the Catalonian superstars to a third match in the tie, eventually losing 5-0 - the start of a long rollercoaster rivalry with the Spanish giants.

This new taste of continental action was lapped up by the Chelsea faithful despite the bruising battles, and the European ties only added to the image of Chelsea as London's most glamorous football club.

TERRY VENABLES

FIXTURE:	FA Cup final
DATE:	20 May 1967
SCORE:	Tottenham Hotspur 2
	Chelsea 1
VENUE:	Wembley
ATTENDANCE:	100,000

#10

Blues Lose Cockney Cup Final

The first FA Cup final to be contested by two teams from London was deservedly won by Tottenham Hotspur, who had too much big-match experience for a Blues side appearing in their club's first ever Wembley final in a major competition.

BOBBY TAMBLING SCORES

Chelsea captain Ron Harris was the final's youngest-ever skipper, but even his leadership skills could not rescue an underwhelming performance from a team which included Tony Hateley, who had signed from Liverpool as a stand-in for the injured Peter Osgood.

Spurs took the lead in the 40th minute with a low right-footed strike from winger Jimmy Robertson, who also helped on a long throw from Dave Mackay for Frank Saul to convert a second.

Bobby Tambling headed a consolation goal in the 85th minute after a cross from the right was missed by Pat Jennings. The result was even harder to take as the Spurs team included former Chelsea stars Jimmy Greaves and Terry Venables.

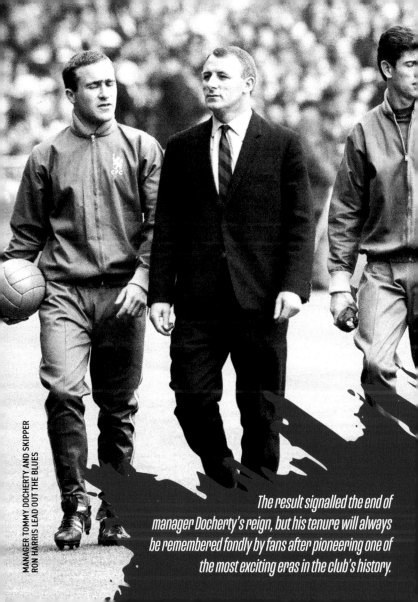

The result signalled the end of manager Docherty's reign, but his tenure will always be remembered fondly by fans after pioneering one of the most exciting eras in the club's history.

*Chelsea's 1970 FA Cup final
against arch-rivals Leeds United ended all square
at 2-2 on a mudbath of a Wembley pitch.*

EDDIE McCREADIE AND LEEDS UNITED
CAPTAIN BILLY BREMNER ON THE LAP OF HONOUR

FIXTURE: FA Cup final

DATE: 11 April 1970

SCORE: Chelsea 2
Leeds United 2

VENUE: Wembley Stadium

ATTENDANCE: 100,000

#11

Blues Earn FA Cup Final Replay

With both teams in the top three of Division One, and considering the fierce rivalry that existed between the clubs, this was always going to be a hard-fought affair.

Leeds were on top for most of the game, with winger Eddie Gray giving Chelsea right-back David Webb a torrid time. The Yorkshire side deservedly took the lead after 20 minutes when Jack Charlton's downward header from a corner failed to bounce on the muddy pitch and the ball dribbled over the line.

Chelsea equalised just before the break when an innocuous shot from winger Peter Houseman rolled under keeper Gary Sprake's body. Leeds appeared to have won the game when an Allan Clarke header hit the post and Mick Jones knocked in the rebound in the 84th minute, but two minutes later, Ian Hutchinson headed in an equaliser from a John Hollins cross.

With no more goals in extra-time, the two squads took a joint lap of honour at the end of the match. The Wembley pitch was in such a dreadful condition after the game that the FA decided to hold the replay at Old Trafford.

IAN HUTCHINSON

FIXTURE:	FA Cup final replay
DATE:	29 April 1970
SCORE:	Chelsea 2
	Leeds United 1
VENUE:	Old Trafford
ATTENDANCE:	62,078

#12

Blues Triumph In Epic Replay

Watched by 28.49 million viewers, the largest-ever UK television audience for a club football match, Chelsea won their first FA Cup final in another bruising encounter.

GOALSCORING HERO DAVID WEBB

Chelsea manager Dave Sexton had astutely moved David Webb into the middle of the defence, while skipper Ron 'Chopper' Harris took care of winger Eddie Gray.

The Whites once again took the lead through a low Mick Jones drive, before Peter Osgood equalised twelve minutes from the end with an iconic diving header from a pinpoint Charlie Cooke cross - creating a record of scoring in every round of the FA Cup.

The game again ended level after 90 minutes, but the cup was won with a goal just before the extra-time break, when one of Ian Hutchinson's trademark long throw-ins was knocked on to the back post, where David Webb was waiting to bundle the ball into the Leeds United net, taking the cup back to Stamford Bridge for the first time.

Thousands of jubilant fans took to the streets the next day to salute their cup-winning heroes as an open-top bus parade along the King's Road concluded with a reception at Fulham Town Hall.

FOOTBALL ASSOCIATION
CHAMPION CUPWINNERS
1955 1970

FOOTBALL LEAGUE CUPWINNERS 1965

Chelsea followed up their
FA Cup final triumph with a Cup Winners' Cup final victory
over Real Madrid in May 1971, also after a replay.

FIXTURE: UEFA Cup Winners' Cup final

DATE: 21 May 1971

SCORE: Chelsea 2
Real Madrid 1

VENUE: Karaiskakis Stadium

ATTENDANCE: 24,000

#13

European Final Success

Peter Osgood, the 'King of Stamford Bridge', put the Blues 1-0 up in the first match, but a 90th-minute Real leveller, after a mistake by John Dempsey, forced a replay following a goalless extra-time.

With the replay to be held two days later on Friday 21 May, many fans slept on Athenian beaches rather than return home and, inspired by the return of Alan Hudson, who had missed the previous year's FA Cup final, and the trickery of winger Charlie Cooke, the team pulled off a historic victory.

Centre-back Dempsey redeemed himself with an emphatic volley, while Ossie made it 2-0 with a low strike into the corner and, even though the Spaniards pulled a goal back through Fleitas 15 minutes before the end, a super save from Peter Bonetti helped Chelsea to become the third London club to win the Cup.

Upon the team's return, the trophy was paraded along the King's Road with a justifiable swagger - the Blues had won two major cup trophies in successive years.

PETER OSGOOD

FIXTURE: UEFA Cup Winners' Cup first round, second leg

DATE: 29 September 1971

SCORE: Chelsea 13
Jeunesse Hautcharage 0

VENUE: Stamford Bridge

ATTENDANCE: 27,621

#14

Biggest Ever European Win

Chelsea scored 13 goals at home for their biggest-ever win in a competitive match. Having already won the first leg 8-0, the aggregate 21-0 scoreline is still a record for a European tie, although it is now held jointly with Feyenoord.

JOHN HOLLINS SCORES FROM THE SPOT

After a hat-trick in the away game, centre-forward Peter Osgood became the fourth Chelsea player to score five goals in a match, after George Hilsdon, Jimmy Greaves and Bobby Tambling.

The game represented a David versus Goliath tussle: the tiny village team from Luxembourg was drawn from a population of fewer than 800 people and included four brothers, a player in glasses and a one-armed striker.

To add injury to insult, their keeper Lucien Fusilier not only picked the ball out of the net 13 times, but also needed three stitches in a head wound after a collision with a goal-hungry Ossie.

PETER OSGOOD SCORES HIS SECOND GOAL OF THE NIGHT

The following morning, the Daily Mirror headline exclaimed 'Chelsea Goal Kings of Europe' with the match described by reporter Nigel Clarke as "more of a massacre than a match".

Chelsea reached their third
cup final in three years after narrowly beating
their London arch-rivals in a pulsating two-legged
League Cup semi-final.

PETER BONETTI GATHERS
THE BALL AHEAD OF TOTTENHAM
HOTSPUR'S ALAN GILZEAN

FIXTURE:	League Cup semi-final, second leg
DATE:	5 January 1972
SCORE:	Tottenham Hotspur 2
	Chelsea 2
VENUE:	White Hart Lane
ATTENDANCE:	52,755

Spurs Edged Out In Epic Cup Clash

#15

Plymouth Argyle, Nottingham Forest, Bolton and Norwich were beaten en route to the clash with the competition's holders, who had beaten Aston Villa in the '71 final.

JOHN HOLLINS

Chelsea took the lead in the first leg at Stamford Bridge through a Peter Osgood curler after 'keeper Pat Jennings and Terry Naylor had collided on the edge of the area, but fell behind after a Naylor header and a superb Martin Chivers volley. Chris Garland's header restored parity before the Blues snatched a late winner through a John Hollins penalty.

Chivers and Garland scored again in the second leg and it looked as though Spurs would take the match into extra-time after Alan Hudson handled the ball in the area and Martin Peters scored from the spot to level the tie at 4-4.

Hudson redeemed himself though, with a low free-kick from out wide, which wrong-footed Jennings and trickled in at the far post to hand the Blues a 5-4 aggregate win. Sadly, Chelsea lost 2-1 to Stoke City in a forgettable Wembley final.

DATE: 7 January 1978

SCORE: Chelsea 4
Liverpool 2

VENUE: Stamford Bridge

ATTENDANCE: 45,449

#16

European
Champions Smashed

While the late 1970s were barren times for Chelsea, beating the reigning European Champions in the third round of the FA Cup was a welcome and memorable highlight.

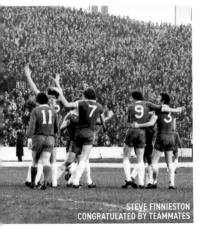

STEVE FINNIESTON
CONGRATULATED BY TEAMMATES

The Reds had not lost at Stamford Bridge for seven years when they arrived for what seemed to them, a routine third-round tie in January 1978, but they were blown away by a thrilling attacking display.

Lightning-fast winger Clive Walker scored early, streaking past Liverpool's Joey Jones and sending a spectacular dipping shot flashing beyond the grasp of England keeper Ray Clemence. The Blues were in total control after Steve Finnieston (on for a limping Charlie Cooke) and Tommy Langley added two more goals in five minutes early in the second half.

Liverpool replied with a goal from David Johnson on the hour, but five minutes later Walker sealed a famous win with a second neat finish. A Kenny Dalglish header on 81 minutes proved to be too little, too late.

Clive Walker, the fastest sprinter on Chelsea's books, ran Joey Jones ragged and the full-back had to be substituted. Ironically, he joined Chelsea in 1982, where his pre-match fist clenching made him a cult hero.

If beating Liverpool in the FA Cup in January 1978 was a surprise, the next FA Cup meeting between the sides was a major shock.

COLIN LEE DOUBLES CHELSEA'S LEAD

FIXTURE:	FA Cup fifth round
DATE:	13 February 1982
SCORE:	Chelsea 2
	Liverpool 0
VENUE:	Stamford Bridge
ATTENDANCE:	41,412

The Blues
Shock The Reds Again

As the teams lined up in February 1982, Chelsea were mid-table in the Second Division, while Liverpool were reigning European champions and league leaders.

Within ten minutes of the start, winger Peter Rhoades-Brown latched on to a loose ball in midfield and, after a clear run at goal, slid the ball past Bruce Grobbelaar for the opener.

The Blues had to endure long spells under great pressure with captain Mickey Droy outstanding in defence and Colin Pates shadowing Reds playmaker Graeme Souness. Six minutes from full-time, a Clive Walker cross caused a mix-up in the Liverpool defence, leaving Colin Lee with a simple tap-in to seal a famous upset.

At the final whistle, thousands of fans ran onto the pitch to celebrate a second FA Cup victory over Bob Paisley's legendary side, who went on to win a domestic double that season, winning both the league title and the league cup.

COLIN LEE MOBBED BY TEAMMATES

DATE: 2 April 1982

EVENT: Chelsea Football Club
Sold for £1

#18

Bates Buys Chelsea Football Club

There is no doubt that Ken Bates, a controversial figure in football, saved Chelsea from possible extinction when he bought the club for just £1 from the Mears family.

KEN CELEBRATES WINNING PROMOTION WITH JOHN HOLLINS, 28 APRIL 1984

Born in London on 4 December 1931, Bates had made his fortune from the ready-mix concrete business and dairy farming before becoming interested in football clubs, briefly serving as Oldham chairman during the 1960s and buying a controlling interest in Wigan in 1980.

When he purchased Chelsea, the club were in serious financial trouble and were languishing in the Second Division. He set about turning the club's fortunes around. After relegation to the Third Division was narrowly avoided in the 1982/83 season, Bates made funds available to manager John Neal to sign players, including Kerry Dixon, David Speedie, Pat Nevin and Nigel Spackman.

By the end of his chairmanship, Stamford Bridge had been substantially modernised, while the team had won several major trophies and were consistently finishing in the top six of the Premier League.

In 2003, Ken Bates sold the club
to Russian oil billionaire Roman Abramovich
for £140 million, although he remained as chairman
until March 2004.

*Winless in nine matches,
Chelsea travelled to Bolton for the penultimate game
of the 1982/83 season knowing that a loss would
probably mean relegation to the third division.*

FIXTURE:	Division Two
DATE:	7 May 1983
SCORE:	Bolton Wanderers 0
	Chelsea 1
VENUE:	Burnden Park
ATTENDANCE:	8,687

#19

Crucial
Victory At Bolton

Clive Walker scored the all-important goal in the pouring Lancashire rain, picking the ball up with his back to goal before turning and smashing it into the top corner.

At the end of the match, the Chelsea players threw their shirts into a jubilant mass of travelling supporters, although, such was the threat of financial collapse at the time, the cost of replacement jerseys was docked from their wages.

The following weekend, Chelsea drew 0-0 with Middlesbrough at Stamford Bridge to complete the great escape, while Wanderers went down, finishing bottom of the Second Division.

Bolton continued to be a happy hunting ground for Chelsea, with Frank Lampard scoring twice at the end of April 2005 to secure a 2-0 victory and the club's first championship for 50 years.

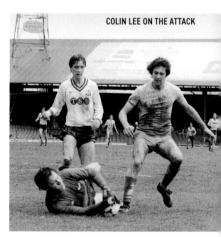

COLIN LEE ON THE ATTACK

FIXTURE:	Division Two
DATE:	27 August 1983
SCORE:	Chelsea 5 Derby County 0
VENUE:	Stamford Bridge
ATTENDANCE:	17,388

#20

Rampant Opening-Day Win

The opening-day thrashing of the Rams signalled the dawn of a new era as Chelsea went on to clinch the 1983/84 Division Two title for the first time in the club's history.

COLIN LEE &
CLIVE WALKER

In a youthful, newly-assembled team in which keeper Eddie Niedzwiecki, midfielders Joe McLaughlin and Nigel Spackman and centre-forward Kerry Dixon were all making their debuts, it was an encouraging sign that the previous season's relegation strugglers were going to be genuine title contenders.

Former club hero John Hollins had returned as player-coach and also started in this classic match. Spackman opened the scoring inside five minutes, while Clive Walker and Chris Hutchins made it three early in the second half.

The scoring was completed with two goals from new striker Dixon, who went on to have a brilliant career as Chelsea's legendary No.9.

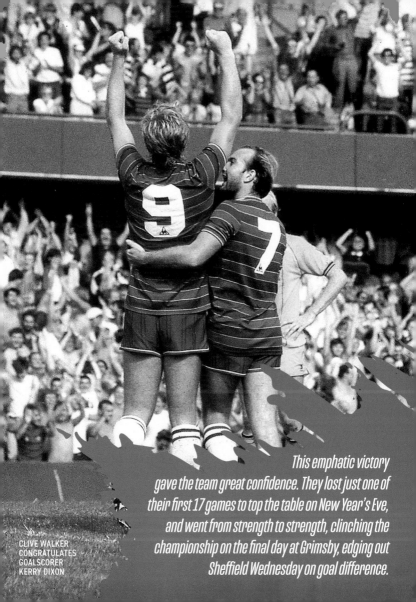

CLIVE WALKER
CONGRATULATES
GOALSCORER
KERRY DIXON

This emphatic victory gave the team great confidence. They lost just one of their first 17 games to top the table on New Year's Eve, and went from strength to strength, clinching the championship on the final day at Grimsby, edging out Sheffield Wednesday on goal difference.

Qualifying as FA Cup runners-up,
Chelsea were back in Europe for the first time
in a generation, playing in the first round of the
Cup Winners' Cup.

DENNIS WISE COLLIDES WITH MICHAEL BILEK

FIXTURE:	UEFA Cup Winners' Cup first round, first leg
DATE:	15 September 1994
SCORE:	Chelsea 4
	Viktoria Zizkov 2
VENUE:	Stamford Bridge
ATTENDANCE:	22,036

#21

Blue Flag Flies In Europe Again

With Manchester United winning the title and qualifying for the Champions League, defeat in the FA Cup final to the Red Devils had a silver lining for the Blues.

Managed by Glenn Hoddle, the Blues were forced to play the little-known Czech team Viktoria Zizkov with a limit on the number of non-English players in the team.

The somewhat inexperienced team flew out of the traps and were two up within four minutes with goals from Paul Furlong and Frank Sinclair. With Chelsea unsure whether to attack or defend this lead, the visitors capitalised on the uncertainty and drew level by half-time. Chelsea were reinvigorated after the break and went ahead through long-range efforts from David Rocastle and Dennis Wise.

Graham Rix, making his debut after moving from Dundee, came on for Rocastle in the last minute, to help secure the first-leg advantage in the tie, which was sealed with a goalless draw a couple of weeks later.

GRAHAM RIX

FIXTURE:	FA Cup final
DATE:	17 May 1997
SCORE:	Chelsea 2
	Middlesbrough 0
VENUE:	Wembley Stadium
ATTENDANCE:	79,160

Sensational

Start To FA Cup Success

Chelsea's fifth FA Cup final could not have got off to a better, or quicker, start with Roberto Di Matteo scoring with a superb long-range shot in the opening minute.

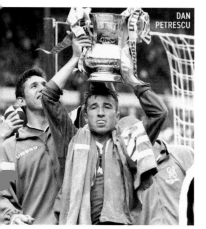

DAN PETRESCU

At that time, it was the quickest-ever Cup final goal, although Everton's Louis Saha broke the record twelve years later in the 2009 Cup final, before Chelsea came back to win the cup 2-1.

Despite Boro's Fabrizio Ravanelli being replaced after only 21 minutes and the Teessiders having a Gianluca Festa goal ruled out before the break, Chelsea were in control overall and sealed victory on 83 minutes when former youth-team player Eddie Newton stabbed home from a flick-on by Gianfranco Zola.

It was the first major honour for many of the Chelsea side, while for centre-forward Mark Hughes, it was his fourth FA Cup final victory after securing three with Manchester United in 1985, 1990 and 1994.

#22

ROBERTO DI MATTEO

After taking over
as Chelsea player-manager in the summer of 1996,
when Glenn Hoddle left the club to manage the England
team, it was the first trophy for newly-appointed boss
Ruud Gullit, who also became the first black coach

FOUR-GOAL GIANLUCA VIALLI

After losing their opening game
of the 1997/98 season at Coventry City, Chelsea
bounced back with their joint-biggest away win in the
Premier League, trouncing Barnsley 6-0 at Oakwell.

FIXTURE: Premier League

DATE: 24 August 1997

SCORE: Barnsley 0
Chelsea 6

VENUE: Oakwell

ATTENDANCE: 18,170

#23

Brilliant Blues Bash Barnsley

The Tykes were playing in the top flight for the first time in their 102-year history, and Chelsea's visit was a striking portent of things to come as they were relegated come May.

Chelsea's joint-biggest away win was also a personal triumph for Gianluca Vialli, who manager Ruud Gullit had chosen as his preferred frontman instead of Mark Hughes.

Vialli repaid the manager's faith with four goals, including a 30-minute hat-trick - the first time he had scored four times in a match. The goals started to flow through Dan Petrescu, who pounced on a defensive error to open the scoring in the 25th minute, while Gustavo Poyet added a second from close range before half-time after his initial header was saved.

Gullit was full of praise for his Italian goalscoring hero, who he said "looked fitter and sharper since he had given up smoking". Ironically, it was Vialli who replaced Gullit in the Chelsea hot-seat, taking over as player-manager in February 1998.

VIALLI CHIPS IN HIS THIRD GOAL

FIXTURE: Premier League

DATE: 6 December 1997

SCORE: Tottenham Hotspur 1
Chelsea 6

VENUE: White Hart Lane

ATTENDANCE: 28,476

#24

Biggest-Ever Win Over Spurs

Level at half-time, Chelsea blew Tottenham Hotspur away in a five-goal second-half blitz to record their biggest-ever win over their North London rivals.

DAN PETRESCU

Wearing yellow socks as part of their blue away kit, Chelsea took the lead late in the first half with a Tore Andre Flo header, but Roman Vega levelled for Spurs just before half-time.

Chelsea took total command in the second half with Roberto Di Matteo heading the Blues back in front followed by a Dan Petrescu lob over keeper Ian Walker. Flo scored his second with an emphatic volley following a neat one-two with Gianfranco Zola, while substitute Mark Nicholls, who had come on for Celestine Babayaro, added a fifth.

Salt was well and truly rubbed in Spurs' wounds when Flo delicately lobbed Walker in stoppage time to complete his hat-trick.

Chelsea had not been beaten at Tottenham for over a decade before this thrashing, and it would not be until November 2006 before Tottenham Hotspur would again taste League victory over the Blues.

TORE ANDRE FLO, ROBERTO DI MATTEO,
GIANFRANCO ZOLA AND EDDIE NEWTON CELEBRATE

*Chelsea and Middlesbrough
had met in the previous season's FA Cup final, and once
again the Blues triumphed by the same scoreline,
this time in the Coca-Cola League Cup final.*

FIXTURE:	Coca-Cola League Cup final
DATE:	29 March 1998
SCORE:	Chelsea 2
	Middlesbrough 0
VENUE:	Wembley Stadium
ATTENDANCE:	77,698

That Déjà Vu Feeling

#25

This would be the first of two major trophies for Chelsea during the 1997/98 season, with the Blues going on to win the UEFA Cup Winners' Cup.

Just as in the FA Cup final the previous year, Roberto Di Matteo was again a goalscorer after an opener by Frank Sinclair. Both goals coming in extra-time.

Sinclair somewhat redeemed himself after having slipped to allow Mark Hughes to score in the 1994 FA Cup final. He started the move in the 95th minute that ended with his header finding the corner of Mark Schwarzer's net. Chelsea's second came in the 107th minute when Boro's defence failed to clear a near-post corner and Di Matteo side-footed the ball into the net on the half-volley.

The trophy was a first feather in the cap for player-manager Gianluca Vialli, who was only weeks into the job having taken over from the departed Ruud Gullit.

FIXTURE: UEFA Cup Winners' Cup semi-final

DATE: 16 April 1998

SCORE: Chelsea 3
Vicenza 1

VENUE: Stamford Bridge

ATTENDANCE: 33,810

#26

Vital Victory Over Vicenza

Having lost the first leg by a single goal in Vicenza, Chelsea looked down and out when the visitors took the lead on the half-hour in the return leg at Stamford Bridge.

GIANFRANCO ZOLA SCORES

But Gus Poyet quickly equalised before half-time when he smashed in a rebound from keeper Pierluigi Brivio, who had made a save from a stinging Gianfranco Zola shot.

Chelsea needed two more goals to go through to the final and were spurred on within minutes of the start of the second half, when player-manager Gianluca Vialli ran down the right wing and sent a pinpoint cross onto the head of fellow countryman Zola.

The best was yet to come. A long drop-kick from stopper Ed de Goey was headed on by striker Mark Hughes, who turned his defender, latched on to his own knock-on and volleyed left-footed past Vicenza's diving keeper.

MARK HUGHES
CELEBRATES HIS
WINNING GOAL

Vialli's spirited side went on to win the Cup by beating Stuttgart in Stockholm, one of three pieces of silverware collected in 1998.

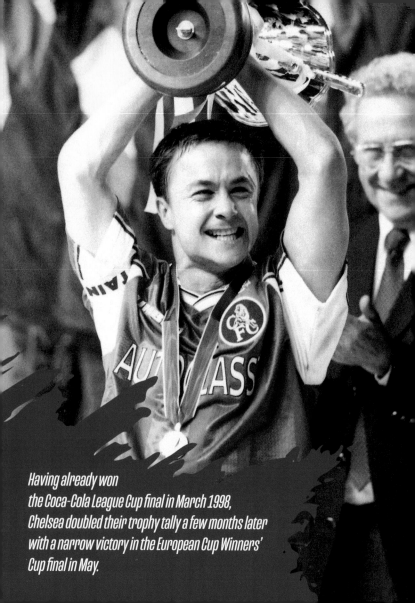

*Having already won
the Coca-Cola League Cup final in March 1998,
Chelsea doubled their trophy tally a few months later
with a narrow victory in the European Cup Winners'
Cup final in May.*

FIXTURE: UEFA Cup Winners' Cup final

DATE: 13 May 1998

SCORE: Chelsea 1
VfB Stuttgart 0

VENUE: Rasunda Stadium

ATTENDANCE: 30,216

#27

Sub Zola
Wins European Final

Chelsea fans turned up in huge numbers in Stockholm to support Gianluca Vialli's exuberant team against German side Stuttgart.

While fans were not treated to a goal feast, the single goal that won Chelsea the second European trophy in their history, was well worth the wait. Feeding on a through-ball from skipper Dennis Wise, the Italian maestro Gianfranco Zola smashed a half-volley past the helpless keeper into the top right-hand corner of the net.

Zola had suffered a rare injury in the run-up to the final, where he was named as substitute. He came on for Tore Andre Flo and within 20 seconds, he scored his wonder-goal, which ultimately was good enough for victory, despite Dan Petrescu being sent off in the 85th minute for an illegal tackle.

Even though he was only on the pitch for less than a quarter of the game, Zola was, not surprisingly, named Man of the Match.

ZOLA SMASHES THE WINNER

FIXTURE:	UEFA Super Cup
DATE:	28 August 1998
SCORE:	Real Madrid 0
	Chelsea 1
VENUE:	Stade Louis II
ATTENDANCE:	9,762

#28

Vialli Wins Third Trophy

Player-manager Gianluca Vialli's Midas touch continued with the addition of the European Super Cup to his CV and the trophy cabinet at Chelsea.

DENNIS WISE & GIANFRANCO ZOLA

Some six months after being appointed, Vialli won the prestigious Super Cup played between the holders of the Cup Winners' Cup and the winners of the UEFA Champions League.

The legendary Real Madrid, then managed by the future FA Cup-winning Chelsea boss Guus Hiddink, were Chelsea's opponents for the game, played for the first time as a one-off match at a neutral ground, the Stade Louis II in Monaco.

The match was settled by a right-footed finish from the edge of the box by Gus Poyet after a pass from the left by Gianfranco Zola. Poyet, who had only come on in the 63rd minute for Roberto Di Matteo, was also named Man of the Match.

GUS POYET CELEBRATES
HIS WINNING GOAL

Vialli was starting to populate the team with foreign players and made history with Chelsea on Boxing Day 1999, when the Blues became the first club to name an all-overseas starting eleven in an English game.

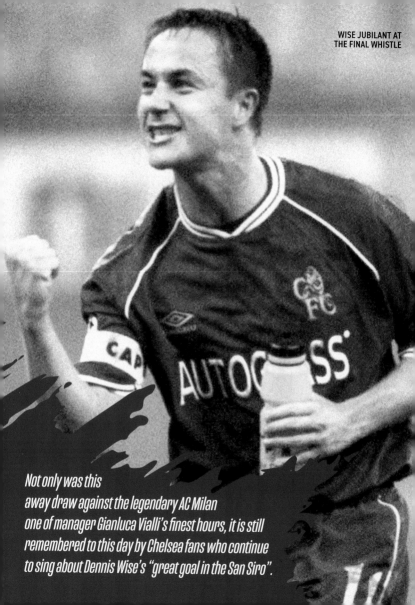

WISE JUBILANT AT
THE FINAL WHISTLE

Not only was this
away draw against the legendary AC Milan
one of manager Gianluca Vialli's finest hours, it is still
remembered to this day by Chelsea fans who continue
to sing about Dennis Wise's "great goal in the San Siro".

FIXTURE:	UEFA Champions League group match
DATE:	26 October 1999
SCORE:	AC Milan 1
	Chelsea 1
VENUE:	Stadio San Siro
ATTENDANCE:	74,855

#29

Wise's 'Great Goal' Seals Draw

This hugely-valuable draw against the European giants left Chelsea needing only a point against group leaders Hertha Berlin at Stamford Bridge to progress.

The German striker Oliver Bierhoff looked to have secured the win for the Italians in the 74th minute when he got in front of defender Frank Leboeuf to clip a header past Ed de Goey.

But Wise hit back three minutes later when he cushioned a through-ball from Roberto Di Matteo on his instep and nutmegged advancing keeper Christian Abbiati to score one of Chelsea's legendary European goals.

Vialli's side were lauded for their attacking intent, forcing AC Milan onto the back foot from the kick-off. Indeed, they could have won the match if Gus Poyet had converted a simple header from six yards out and Tore Andre Flo had not missed an open goal from a Wise cross, which he scooped over the bar.

WISE SCORES HIS LEGENDARY GOAL.

FIXTURE:	Premier League
DATE:	3 October 1999
SCORE:	Chelsea 5
	Manchester United 0
VENUE:	Stamford Bridge
ATTENDANCE:	34,909

#30

Blues Crush
Treble-Winners

Reigning European champions and treble-winners Manchester United suffered their biggest-ever defeat to Chelsea after having been unbeaten for ten months.

POYET OPENS THE SCORING

Within 27 seconds of referee Dermot Gallagher blowing his whistle on a sunny autumnal afternoon, Gus Poyet had flicked a header past hapless keeper Massimo Taibi for the opening goal.

Chris Sutton, who had been receiving some stick from Chelsea fans as he had yet to score in the league, got on the wrong side of Henning Berg to nod a header past a despairing Taibi in the 16th minute. A few minutes later, United were down to ten men when Nicky Butt reacted to a Dennis Wise challenge. With both players on the ground, Wise slyly pinched Butt's leg. Angrily, Butt responded with a knee to the midriff, earning himself a red card in the process.

United disintegrated with Poyet scoring a second, while Berg slid a low Gianfranco Zola cross into his own net as the tragicomedy continued.

JODY MORRIS NETS NUMBER FIVE

With ten minutes remaining,
20-year-old Jody Morris, on as a substitute, found
himself alone in the box and fired a rare goal through
Taibi's legs. A famous five-star win for Chelsea,
which also knocked United off the top of the table.

Chelsea secured their
second FA Cup in four years with a narrow victory
over Aston Villa, in the last final to be played at the
old Wembley Stadium.

FIXTURE: FA Cup final

DATE: 20 May 2000

SCORE: Chelsea 1
Aston Villa 0

VENUE: Wembley Stadium

ATTENDANCE: 78,217

#31

Di Matteo Strikes Again

Once again Roberto Di Matteo scored, as he had done against Middlesbrough in the 1997 Wembley final, but this time, his was the only goal needed to lift the FA Cup.

Chelsea were deserved winners in a game of few chances, most of which were missed by George Weah, with Dennis Wise also having a goal disallowed for offside. The current England manager Gareth Southgate also headed wide a rare chance for the Villans.

In the 73rd minute, Chelsea struck. After an error by Villa keeper David James, who fumbled a free-kick from Gianfranco Zola, Di Matteo pounced and blasted the loose ball high into the roof of the net. Villa's best chance to get back into the match fell to Benito Carbone, but his tame shot failed to test Ed de Goey.

Manager Gianluca Vialli's winning streak continued and culminated with his fifth trophy when Manchester United were beaten in the FA Charity Shield in August 2000, although he parted ways with the club five games into the new season after an indifferent start.

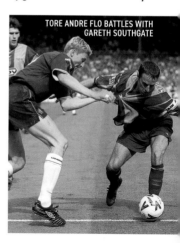

TORE ANDRE FLO BATTLES WITH GARETH SOUTHGATE

FIXTURE: Premier League

DATE: 11 May 2003

SCORE: Chelsea 2
Liverpool 1

VENUE: Stamford Bridge

ATTENDANCE: 41,911

#32

Champions League Place Secured

Chelsea just needed to stay ahead of Liverpool on the final day of the season to qualify for the lucrative Champions League.

MARCEL DESAILLY MOBBED BY TEAMMATES AFTER HIS EQUALISER

The fixture list created a dramatic denouement as Liverpool were Chelsea's opponents at Stamford Bridge, and all the Blues needed to do was get a draw to stay in fourth place.

To add to the tension, the visitors scored first through Sami Hyypia in the eleventh minute when he headed home a Danny Murphy free-kick. Liverpool's lead lasted just a minute though, with winger Jesper Gronkjaer sending in a cross for Marcel Desailly to head in off Jerzy Dudek's post. It was Gronkjaer who fired Chelsea ahead when he brushed past John-Arne Riise's weak challenge and curled a delicious shot around Dudek's despairing dive.

To make matters even worse for Liverpool, Steven Gerrard was shown a second yellow card for a reckless challenge on Graeme Le Saux in the 88th minute.

Gronkjaer's winner is often falsely described as being worth some £20 million to Chelsea although Desailly's goal would have been enough to earn the financial rewards that came from the Champions League.

The future of
Chelsea Football Club changed
forever, and for the better, when Russian businessman
Roman Abramovich bought the Blues from Ken Bates
on 1 July 2003.

#33

Roman Conquest

The new owner cleared the club's debt and started to bring top talent to the club including Damien Duff, Joe Cole, Hernan Crespo and Claude Makelele.

The fans responded by clapping along enthusiastically to the Russian folk song Kalinka that was played before games at the Bridge. Improvements were evident straight away, with the team finishing second in the league under Claudio Ranieri and reaching the semi-final of the Champions League. The catalyst that helped take the Blues to the next level was the arrival of the 'Special One', Jose Mourinho, who in his first spell with the club won two Premier Leagues, the FA Cup and the League Cup twice.

Mourinho's departure triggered the arrival of a succession of high-profile managers from Avram Grant to Rafa Benitez before Jose returned for a second spell. The trophies continued to arrive throughout Abramovich's tenure, and even after Mourinho departed, Chelsea won the Premier League under Antonio Conte and the Europa League under Maurizio Sarri.

Club legend Frank Lampard helped bring youth players into the first team before former PSG manager Thomas Tuchel arrived in January 2021 to win the Champions League for the second time in the club's history. The ambition to be the best still burns under Abramovich's ownership as he looks to improve his tally of 17 major trophies in 18 years.

FIXTURE:	Premier League
DATE:	17 August 2003
SCORE:	Liverpool 1
	Chelsea 2
VENUE:	Anfield
ATTENDANCE:	44,082

#34

Reds Routed Under Roman

The dawn of the Roman Abramovich era saw the Blues win their first Premier League match after the Russian businessman's takeover, against Liverpool at Anfield.

JUAN SEBASTIAN VERON'S OPENER

The Blues gave league debuts to a number of expensive signings including Damien Duff, Claude Makelele and Juan Sebastian Veron, who thundered a great finish past Jerzy Dudek from a Jesper Gronkjaer cross.

Liverpool luckily equalised through a twice-taken Michael Owen penalty after the star striker had missed his first effort: referee Steve Bennett ordered it to be retaken because Carlo Cudicini had moved off his line despite Owen sending his low shot hopelessly wide.

But it was veteran forward Jimmy Floyd Hasselbaink, who had come on for Eidur Gudjohnsen at half-time, who sealed the win with a low shot that crept in at the far post, prompting him to remove his shirt and swirl it around his head in jubilation.

JIMMY FLOYD HASSELBAINK CELEBRATES HIS WINNER WITH JESPER GRONKJAER

This pivotal win fired a warning to the Blues' title rivals that the support and investment of Abramovich would make Chelsea Football Club a force to be reckoned with.

Chelsea had not beaten Arsenal
in 16 attempts over five years before the London rivals
met in the Champions League quarter-final in 2004.

FIXTURE:	UEFA Champions League quarter-final, second leg
DATE:	6 April 2004
SCORE:	Arsenal 1
	Chelsea 2
VENUE:	Highbury
ATTENDANCE:	35,486

#35

Late Bridge Goal Sinks Gunners

The sides had drawn 1-1 in the first leg at the Bridge and it looked as though history would repeat itself at Highbury, until Wayne Bridge's late winner at the Clock End.

The England defender rifled home a left-foot finish after a neat one-two with Eidur Gudjohnsen to send the travelling supporters into ecstasy.

In an enthralling match, Jose Antonio Reyes gave Arsenal the lead from close range in first-half injury-time. Super Frank Lampard scored an equaliser within six minutes of the restart after Claude Makelele's long-range strike was spilled by Jens Lehmann. With the scores level, both sides became understandably cautious, although Ashley Cole made a goalline clearance at full stretch from Gudjohnsen in the 85th minute.

Bridge popped up two minutes later to win the tie, which is fondly remembered as one of the great Chelsea away 'European' nights. Sadly, Chelsea fell at the semi-final hurdle to Monaco, contributing to the end of manager Claudio Ranieri's tenure.

WAYNE BRIDGE'S LATE WINNER

DATE: 2 June 2004

EVENT: Jose Mourinho becomes manager of Chelsea FC

#36

Chelsea Welcome The Special One

Within a year of Roman Abramovich arriving, Chelsea appointed Jose Mourinho with the mission of turning the Blues into the best team in England and Europe.

Fresh from lifting the Champions League trophy with Porto, Jose had the confidence to exclaim at his unveiling: "Please don't say I'm arrogant, because what I say is true. I am European champion, so I'm not one of the bottle. I think I'm a special one."

He certainly lived up to his words and in his first season, the club won the League for the first time in 50 years, setting records along the way for the most wins, most home and away wins, fewest goals conceded and most points.

With the solid spine to the team made up of such players as Petr Cech, John Terry, Frank Lampard and Didier Drogba, the Blues became virtually unstoppable, and the trophy cabinet filled up with two Premier League titles in a row, an FA Cup and two League Cups in Jose's three seasons at the club.

His detailed analysis of the opposition, tactically astute formations and calculated mind games, turned Chelsea into a major European force, and although he left the club after an indifferent start to the 2007/08 season, the Mourinho story still had more chapters to come at Chelsea.

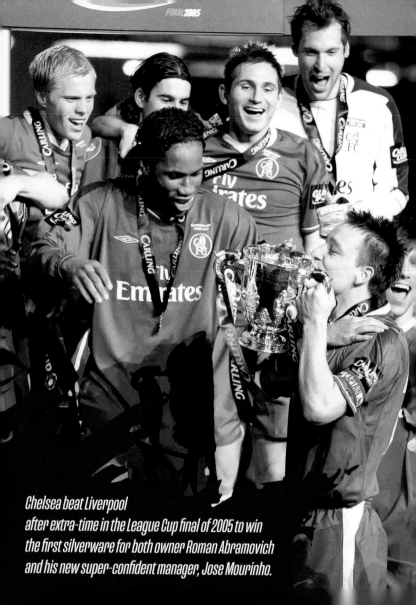

Chelsea beat Liverpool after extra-time in the League Cup final of 2005 to win the first silverware for both owner Roman Abramovich and his new super-confident manager, Jose Mourinho.

FIXTURE:	League Cup final
DATE:	27 February 2005
SCORE:	Chelsea 3
	Liverpool 2
VENUE:	Millennium Stadium
ATTENDANCE:	71,662

#37

First Trophy For Roman & Jose

Liverpool could not have got off to a better, or more dramatic, start with John Arne Riise scoring within the first minute with a stunning left-foot volley from a Fernando Morientes cross - the fastest goal in League Cup final history.

Chelsea levelled the scores after 78 minutes when Steven Gerrard - the subject of speculation that Chelsea were interested in buying him - headed a Paulo Ferreira free-kick into his own net.

Following the goal, Blues boss Jose Mourinho was sent off for taunting the Liverpool fans by putting his fingers to his lips, which he claimed afterwards was aimed at the media. It wasn't until the 17th minute of extra-time that Didier Drogba put the Blues ahead, stabbing home from close range after a Glen Johnson throw-in.

With eight minutes left, when Mateja Kezman extended Chelsea's lead from an Eidur Gudjohnsen cross, greatly helped by a Jerzy Dudek fumble, the Blues looked home and dry, but the drama didn't stop there. A minute later Antonio Nunez outjumped Cech to head home and make for a tense finale. Despite Liverpool's frantic efforts, Chelsea held on to secure their third League Cup win.

KEZMAN PUTS THE BLUES 3-1 UP

FIXTURE:	UEFA Champions League, round of 16
DATE:	8 March 2005
SCORE:	Chelsea 4 Barcelona 2
VENUE:	Stamford Bridge
ATTENDANCE:	41,515

#38

Blues Beat Barca In Classic

Needing to win the second leg of this round of 16 Champions League tie after a first-leg loss in Spain, Chelsea raced into a 3-0 lead within 20 minutes of the start.

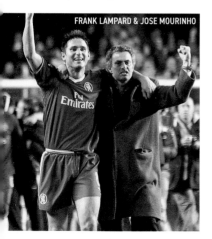

FRANK LAMPARD & JOSE MOURINHO

With only seven minutes gone, Eidur Gudjohnsen collected a pass from Mateja Kezman and turned his man before firing a rising shot past the onrushing Barcelona keeper Victor Valdes.

Nine minutes later, the advantage was doubled. Frank Lampard reacted first to turn in Joe Cole's saved shot, and when Damien Duff raced onto a Cole through-ball before sliding it between the legs of Valdez, it looked as if the tie was over.

But Ronaldinho had other ideas. After scoring from the penalty spot following a needless handball by Paulo Ferreira, he showed his world-class brilliance, conjuring a second goal out of nothing, flashing a shot from a static start past a bamboozled Petr Cech. Chelsea now needed to score a fourth.

With 15 minutes to go, the Catalan giants were going through until Chelsea captain John Terry met a Duff corner with a towering header steered inside the far post to clinch a place in the quarter-finals.

FRANK LAMPARD CELEBRATES HIS GOAL THAT SECURED THE LEAGUE TITLE WITH WILLIAM GALLAS AND DIDIER DROGBA

This fixture had been identified by manager Jose Mourinho as the one in which Chelsea could end their 50-year wait to become champions again, but they were up against a physical Bolton side chasing a European place of their own.

FIXTURE:	Premier League
DATE:	30 April 2005
SCORE:	Bolton Wanderers 0
	Chelsea 2
VENUE:	Reebok Stadium
ATTENDANCE:	27,653

#39

Premier League Champions

Chelsea sealed their first championship for 50 years with an away victory at Bolton Wanderers thanks to a second-half brace from Blues legend Frank Lampard.

Chelsea had to be at their resolute best as Sam Allardyce's side dominated the first half, with Petr Cech in inspired form to keep out Stelios Giannakopoulos and Gary Speed.

Sensing their opportunity, the Blues improved in the second half and took the lead after an hour when Frank Lampard latched onto Didier Drogba's flick-on and smashed his finish past Jussi Jaaskelainen, prompting wild celebrations from visiting players and fans alike. Lampard capped a classic afternoon 16 minutes later by coolly rounding the keeper and slotting the ball into an empty net.

Chelsea finished the season twelve points clear of second-placed Arsenal, having lost only one league game and conceded just 15 goals throughout the season - still a record to this day.

TERRY, ABRAMOVICH & LAMPARD

FIXTURE:	Premier League
DATE:	29 April 2006
SCORE:	Chelsea 3 Manchester United 0
VENUE:	Stamford Bridge
ATTENDANCE:	42,219

#40

Blues Thrash
Red Devils To Win Title

Just a point was required to clinch back-to-back Premier League titles when famous foes, Manchester United, came to the Bridge on a sunny spring afternoon in 2006.

A tough tackle by Frank Lampard on Cristiano Ronaldo won Chelsea an early corner, which Super Frank placed on the head of Didier Drogba. The striker flicked the ball on for William Gallas, virtually on the goalline, to nod in with just five minutes on the clock.

Wayne Rooney missed a sitter after being put clean through on goal, before Joe Cole, on the hour mark, showed him how to do it properly, collecting a flick-on from Drogba, beating Nemanja Vidic and Rio Ferdinand on the turn, and slamming home past Edwin van der Sar.

The third goal was also a collector's item. After breaking up a United attack in his own penalty area, Ricardo Carvalho ran the length of the pitch to receive the ball just inside the United box and smashed a right-footed drive past van der Sar. Drogba and Carvalho celebrated by smoking imaginary cigars in front of the jubilant Chelsea fans.

WILLIAM GALLAS CELEBRATES HIS GOAL

Chelsea's title party started in earnest at the final whistle and even Manchester United manager Sir Alex Ferguson was magnanimous in defeat: "We had a lot of the play and made some good chances, but we didn't make it count. But Chelsea deserve all the plaudits they will get and, especially on their home form, they are worthy champions."

*Behind after an early goal
from 17-year-old Theo Walcott, Chelsea fought back
with two typical strikes from Didier Drogba to earn their
fourth Football League Cup trophy and their second
in three years under Jose Mourinho.*

FIXTURE:	League Cup final
DATE:	25 February 2007
SCORE:	Chelsea 2
	Arsenal 1
VENUE:	Millennium Stadium
ATTENDANCE:	70,073

Chelsea Win Fourth League Cup

#41

Drogba was maybe fortunate not to be given offside for his first goal, after Michael Ballack played him in for the striker to slip the ball under Manuel Almunia.

Arsenal manager Arsene Wenger spent most of the rest of the first half upset about the linesman's failure to raise his flag. Arsenal looked the more likely team to win after the break, especially when Blues captain John Terry was knocked unconscious by a boot in the face as he tried to finish off an Arjen Robben corner.

The injury fired up the Chelsea players, and in the 84th minute Drogba, probably the most dangerous centre-forward in the country at that time, flicked a header past Almunia and into the corner of the net from a Robben cross.

The match ended in unsavoury fashion when Kolo Toure prompted an ugly scuffle after clashing with John Mikel Obi, that referee Howard Webb deemed worthy of three red cards, Arsenal's Toure and Emmanuel Adebayor getting their marching orders, as well as Obi.

FIXTURE:	FA Cup final
DATE:	19 May 2007
SCORE:	Chelsea 1 Manchester United 0
VENUE:	Wembley Stadium
ATTENDANCE:	89,826

#42

Drogba Wins Cup At New Wembley

The first ever FA Cup final at the new Wembley Stadium ended in a narrow victory for the Blues after an almost inevitable Didier Drogba moment of brilliance.

JOHN TERRY

The two best sides in the country produced a game that will not live long in football purists' memories, but that did not bother Chelsea, who added the FA Cup to the League Cup they had won earlier in the season.

Rio Ferdinand and Nemanja Vidic had largely contained Didier Drogba over 90 minutes, with the cup talisman limited to a curling free-kick that clipped the outside of the post. Indeed, Vidic could have won the game for the Red Devils with the last touch of normal time, but his glancing header from Ryan Giggs' in-swinging free-kick was marginally too high.

Both teams had glorious chances in extra-time. Giggs picked out Petr Cech with the goal at his mercy while Salomon Kalou put a curling shot just past the post with Edwin van der Sar scrambling across his line.

It was left to Drogba and
Frank Lampard to exchange a telepathic one-two
that left the Golden Boot winner to beat the onrushing
van der Sar with a deft chip. At his best,
Drogba was now unstoppable and unplayable.

*Having already pipped
Chelsea to the league title on the season's final day,
Manchester United were now heading into extra-time
with the Blues in the Champions League title decider,
after Frank Lampard had cancelled out Cristiano
Ronaldo's opener.*

FRANK LAMPARD LEVELS THE SCORE

FIXTURE: Champions League final

DATE: 21 May 2008

SCORE: Chelsea 1
Manchester United 1

United won 6-5
on penalties

VENUE: Luzhniki Stadium

ATTENDANCE: 67,310

#43

Champions League Title So Close

Chelsea were an agonising John Terry slip and a post width's away from winning the most important game in the club's history.

Didier Drogba had been sent off four minutes from the end of extra-time after slapping Nemanja Vidic. In the penalty shoot-out, Ronaldo had missed Manchester United's third spot-kick, which allowed Terry the chance to win the trophy for his beloved Blues with the fifth penalty.

Captain Fantastic lost his footing on the wet pitch and, even though he sent Edwin van der Sar the wrong way, his mis-hit shot struck the outside of the post and went wide.

Van der Sar then saved Nicolas Anelka's sudden-death penalty. If Drogba had stayed on the pitch, he may well have taken the fifth penalty. Such is the cruel hand of fate.

DROGBA & RIO FERDINAND

FIXTURE:	FA Cup final
DATE:	30 May 2009
SCORE:	Chelsea 2
	Everton 1
VENUE:	Wembley Stadium
ATTENDANCE:	89,391

#44

Frank Gives Guus Farewell Cup Win

Chelsea's fifth FA Cup final win came thanks to a stunning strike from Frank Lampard, presenting interim boss Guus Hiddink with the perfect leaving present.

RAY WILKINS & GUUS HIDDINK

Dutchman Guus Hiddink, the manager of the Russian national team, had stepped in to manage Chelsea after Luiz Felipe Scolari had been relieved of his duties with three months of the season remaining.

After securing a commendable third-place finish in the league, Chelsea comfortably won the FA Cup against Everton to give their popular manager a fairytale finish to his time in charge. The Toffees made a dream start. When a Pienaar ball from the left was half-cleared, Marouane Fellaini headed the ball down and into Saha's path, who smashed it past the despairing Petr Cech after just 25 seconds - the quickest goal in FA Cup final history.

The Blues came back strongly and equalised through Didier Drogba, reacting first to an inviting Florent Malouda cross, with his trademark header beating a stationary Tim Howard.

In the 72nd minute,
despite slipping before he shot, Frank Lampard let fly
from long range, his rising shot stinging Tim Howard's
fingertips on its way into the corner for the winner.
The scoreline could have been more emphatic
if a Malouda shot, that looked to have crossed the line
after hitting the bar, had been given.

With Didier Drogba back to
his lethal best and Frank Lampard enjoying a prolific
vein of scoring form, title rivals Liverpool, Arsenal and
Manchester United had been beaten home and away.

FIXTURE: Premier League

DATE: 9 May 2010

SCORE: Chelsea 8
Wigan Athletic 0

VENUE: Stamford Bridge

ATTENDANCE: 41,383

#45

Blues Thump
Wigan To Win Title

Appointed manager in the summer of 2009, regaining the Premier League after three fruitless seasons was the top priority for serial winner Carlo Ancelotti.

Come the final day, Ancelotti's side just needed victory over Wigan to end Manchester United's three-season reign as champions. Once Nicolas Anelka had drilled a finish past Mike Pollitt at his near post in the sixth minute, the result looked inevitable.

Wigan's cause was not helped by the first-half dismissal of defender Gary Caldwell for pulling down Frank Lampard. Super Frank placed the resulting penalty in the bottom corner. The second half rained goals through Salomon Kalou, a second from Anelka, a Drogba hat-trick, including a penalty which Lampard generously let him take, and, to put the icing on the cake, a rare Ashley Cole volley.

The thumping win against Roberto Martinez's hopelessly outclassed side was the biggest in Chelsea's 105-year league history and saw the Blues break the record for the most goals in a Premier League season with 103.

FIXTURE:	FA Cup final
DATE:	15 May 2010
SCORE:	Chelsea 1
	Portsmouth 0
VENUE:	Wembley Stadium
ATTENDANCE:	88,335

#46

Chelsea
At The Double

Chelsea sealed their historic first Premier League and FA Cup double with a one-sided victory over Portsmouth at Wembley Stadium.

Didier Drogba's side-footed free-kick just before the hour mark was the only goal in an incident-packed game that saw Chelsea hit the woodwork five times and both sides miss from the penalty spot.

Drogba kept up his remarkable record of scoring in each of his six games at Wembley with his 37th goal of the season. His side-footed free-kick strike going in off David James' left-hand post only minutes after Kevin-Prince Boateng's scuffed penalty had been saved by Petr Cech, a rare chance in a one-sided match in which Frank Lampard, John Terry, Salomon Kalou and Drogba, on two occasions, all struck the frame of the goal.

Lampard also had the luxury of a rare penalty miss in the closing minutes when he was brought down by Michael Brown, but shot wide from the spot.

DROGBA STRIKES FOR GOAL

The narrow victory capped a sensational season for Carlo Ancelotti, who won the double in his first season in charge; and was also a personal triumph for Ashley Cole, who became the most decorated player in FA Cup history by picking up his sixth winner's medal.

Chelsea won the FA Cup final for the seventh time in their history with talisman Didier Drogba scoring the winner once more as they overcame old foes Liverpool at Wembley.

FIXTURE:	FA Cup final
DATE:	5 May 2012
SCORE:	Chelsea 2
	Liverpool 1
VENUE:	Wembley Stadium
ATTENDANCE:	89,102

Drogba Does It Again

Didier Drogba's cross-shot goal early in the second half, his fourth in the Wembley showpiece, proved decisive, although Petr Cech's miraculous save from an Andy Carroll header late on, did not go unnoticed.

Liverpool keeper Pepe Reina had been badly at fault for the first goal when he let Ramires score at the near post after he had dispossessed Jay Spearing.

After falling two behind when Drogba struck after the break, Liverpool brought on Andy Carroll for Spearing, sparking the Reds into life, and eight minutes after his introduction, the striker pulled a goal back when he turned John Terry in the area and fired high into the roof of the net.

The hard-fought win enhanced stand-in manager Roberto Di Matteo's claim to become the permanent successor to Andre Villas-Boas, an ambition that became a reality when the Blues won their first Champions League final a couple of weeks later.

DROGBA HITS THE WINNER

#47

FIXTURE: UEFA Champions League final

DATE: 19 May 2012

SCORE: Chelsea 1
Bayern Munich 1

Chelsea won 4-3
on penalties

VENUE: Allianz Arena

ATTENDANCE: 62,500

Champions Of Europe, At Last!

After falling behind to a fortuitous Thomas Muller header in the 83rd minute, Didier Drogba powered a header past Manuel Neuer to take the match into extra-time.

DIDIER DROGBA
& PETR CECH
CELEBRATE

With former Chelsea star Arjen Robben having an extra-time spot-kick saved by Petr Cech, the final was to be decided by penalties for the first time since 2008, when Chelsea had lost to Manchester United.

The teams were level after three successful spot-kicks each, when Man of the Match Cech tipped Bastian Schweinsteiger's penalty onto a post to leave the Blues one kick away from glory.

After Drogba had been sent off in the 2008 final, John Terry stood in as Chelsea's fifth penalty taker, only to see his shot hit the outside of the post after he slipped on his run-up.

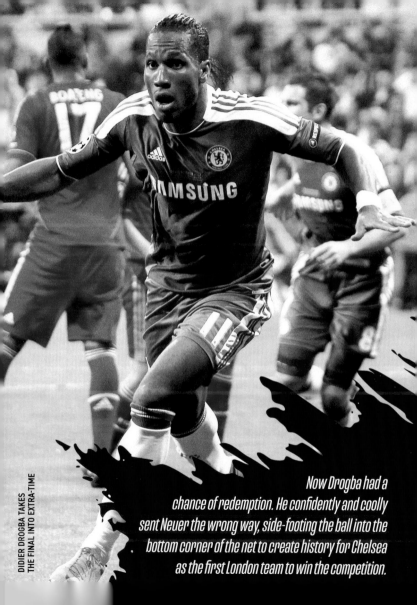

Now Drogba had a chance of redemption. He confidently and coolly sent Neuer the wrong way, side-footing the ball into the bottom corner of the net to create history for Chelsea as the first London team to win the competition.

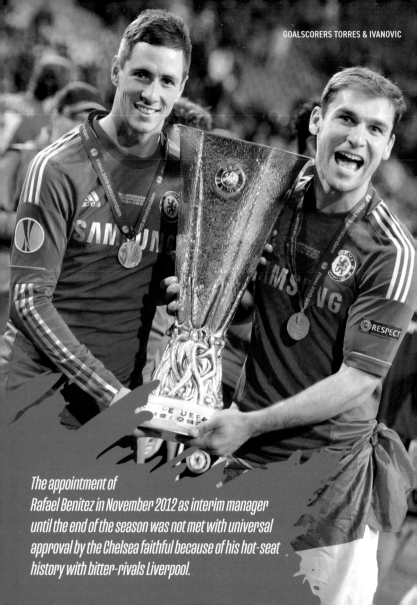

The appointment of Rafael Benitez in November 2012 as interim manager until the end of the season was not met with universal approval by the Chelsea faithful because of his hot-seat history with bitter-rivals Liverpool.

FIXTURE: UEFA Europa League final

DATE: 15 May 2013

SCORE: Benfica 1
Chelsea 2

VENUE: Amsterdam ArenA

ATTENDANCE: 46,163

#49

Rafa Wins Europa League

By the end of his reign, Rafa had won the fans' respect and gratitude with a respectable third-place league finish and the Europa League trophy.

Chelsea took the lead against the run of play just before the hour through ex-Liverpool striker Fernando Torres, who rounded keeper Artur to chip in from the tightest of angles.

Benfica drew level from the spot after Cesar Azpilicueta had handled Eduardo Salvio's header, Oscar Cardozo slamming the ball to the right of Cech, who had dived the other way. Frank Lampard nearly gave Chelsea the lead with three minutes remaining, but his curling 20-yard drive hit the bar and bounced back out to safety. The dramatic conclusion came deep into stoppage time when Branislav Ivanovic - suspended for the previous year's Champions League final - rose to meet Juan Mata's corner and send a looping header into the far corner of the net.

The Blues had become only the fourth club to win all three major UEFA club titles, and it was a fitting way for Benitez to bow out with his head held high.

IVANOVIC'S HEADED WINNER

FIXTURE: Premier League

DATE: 22 March 2014

SCORE: Chelsea 6
Arsenal 0

VENUE: Stamford Bridge

ATTENDANCE: 41,614

#50

Chelsea Slam Six Past The Gunners

Arsene Wenger will want to forget his 1,000th game in charge, as his Arsenal side were crushed by Chelsea - the biggest victory in the history of the capital's oldest top-flight derby.

The result marked the most goals that Chelsea had scored against Arsenal, the club's biggest margin of victory over the Gunners and the joint-heaviest margin of defeat suffered by Wenger at Arsenal.

The league leaders took just seven minutes to establish a two-goal lead with Samuel Eto'o and Andre Schurrle shooting past Wojciech Szczesny. Eden Hazard then converted a penalty after Alex Oxlade-Chamberlain had handled the ball on the line. Referee Andre Marriner wrongly sent off Kieran Gibbs for the offence, despite Oxlade-Chamberlain confessing he was the culprit. Three minutes before the break Chelsea extended their lead as Fernando Torres created a simple tap-in for Oscar.

After the interval, Oscar scored a second with a shot that bounced over Szczesny's hapless dive, while substitute Mo Salah completed the demolition with his first Blues goal.

HAZARD WITH NUMBER THREE

ANDRE SCHURRLE CELEBRATES

Jose Mourinho masterminded victory over Arsene Wenger in his 500th game in charge of Arsenal in 2005, and now he had ruined his big day once again.

An Eden Hazard header was enough to give Jose Mourinho his third Premier League title, having spent a record 274 days at the top of the table.

FIXTURE:	Premier League
DATE:	3 May 2015
SCORE:	Chelsea 1
	Crystal Palace 0
VENUE:	Stamford Bridge
ATTENDANCE:	41,566

Mourinho's Hat-Trick

The cagey Sunday afternoon derby victory sent the Blues 16 points clear and beyond the reaches of the chasing Manchester pack.

The deadlock was broken right on half-time when Eden Hazard surged into the area and went down under a James McArthur challenge. His penalty was easily saved by Julian Speroni, but the rebound flew up for the PFA Player of the Year to head it back across the stranded keeper and into the far corner of the net.

After the break, Chelsea were content to keep the ball and run down the clock, with the only major scare coming from Jason Puncheon who fired just wide with Thibaut Courtois beaten. Chelsea held on to give master strategist Mourinho his third title as Chelsea manager, vindicating owner Roman Abramovich's decision to bring him back to the Bridge.

At the end of a record-breaking season, skipper John Terry became the first player since Gary Pallister to play in every minute of a title-winning campaign.

EDEN HAZARD

FIXTURE:	FA Women's Cup final
DATE:	1 August 2015
SCORE:	Chelsea FC Women 1
	Notts County Ladies 0
VENUE:	Wembley Stadium
ATTENDANCE:	30,710

#52

Chelsea FC
Women Do The Double

The year 2015 was a stellar one for Chelsea FC Women as they won the FA Women's Cup at Wembley and became FA Women's Super League champions for the first time.

JI SO-YUN SQUEEZES HOME THE WINNER

The August showpiece match was the first women's final to be staged at Wembley and was watched by a record crowd of 30,710, and a BBC television audience of nearly two million.

After a quiet start, Chelsea winger and Player of the Match Eniola Aluko raised the tempo, firing in a couple of great efforts on goal, before turning provider, weaving her way through the County defence and cleverly supplying South Korean centre-forward Ji So-yun inside the box to toe-poke the ball home from close-range.

Emma Hayes' team hunted for a second goal, but in the end the lone first-half strike proved enough to set the Blues up for a historic double.

CAPTAIN KATIE CHAPMAN
WITH TEAMMATES & TROPHY

*Chelsea duly won
the league in October, two points ahead
of Manchester City, to clinch their first WSL title
and a League and cup double.*

*Chelsea were crowned
league champions for the sixth time under new manager
Antonio Conte following substitute Michy Batshuayi's
late close-range winner at the Hawthorns.*

FIXTURE:	Premier League
DATE:	12 May 2017
SCORE:	WBA 0 Chelsea 1
VENUE:	The Hawthorns
ATTENDANCE:	25,367

#53

King Conte Reigns Supreme

Belgian striker Batshuayi came off the bench to break through a stubborn Albion defence with a neat poacher's goal to seal the title with two games to spare.

Chelsea had the bulk of the attacking play, with Victor Moses forcing the best save of the night early in the second half, but the Baggies put plenty of bodies behind the ball to thwart the visitors.

The forwards struggled to find a spark, with Eden Hazard hitting a long-range shot that went out for a corner, before Conte introduced Batshuayi and Willian for Hazard and Pedro with 15 minutes left. His masterstroke paid dividends, as had his crucial switch to a three-man defence in September that turned Chelsea's season around and started a run of 13 straight league wins.

The mainstay of Conte's team was the tough-tackling midfield dynamo N'Golo Kante, who became the first player to win the Premier League with two different clubs in consecutive seasons, having won the title with Leicester City the previous campaign.

KING CONTE

FIXTURE:	Premier League
DATE:	21 May 2017
SCORE:	Chelsea 5 Sunderland 1
VENUE:	Stamford Bridge
ATTENDANCE:	41,618

#54

Legend John Terry's Farewell

Champions Chelsea became the first side to register 30 victories in a Premier League season with this comfortable, final-day win over bottom club Sunderland, in which they said farewell to club captain, leader and legend John Terry.

TERRY HANDS THE CAPTAIN'S
ARMBAND TO GARY CAHILL

Unexpectedly, the Blues, who had sealed their sixth top-flight title nine days earlier, fell behind to a Javier Manquillo volley in the third minute, but hit back five minutes later through Man of the Match Willian. The game came to an emotional halt in the 26th minute for Terry, who had worn the number 26 throughout his career at the club, to be substituted and leave the field in tears to a guard of honour from his teammates.

The game remained level until Eden Hazard lashed in his 17th goal of the season across Jordan Pickford to give the Blues the lead on the hour, before his replacement, Pedro, pounced on a poor header from Joleon Lescott to nod into an empty net.

Another substitute, Michy Batshuayi, put the cherry on top with a brace in added-on time to send Chelsea to Wembley for the FA Cup final with their spirits high.

*At the end of the match,
an emotional Terry lifted the Premier League trophy,
the 15th major trophy the 36-year-old had won at
Chelsea since his debut in October 1998*

With manager Emma Hayes advised not to travel because of her pregnancy, Chelsea FC Women clinched the Women's Super League title and a domestic double with a hard-fought victory against Bristol City Women.

FIXTURE:	Women's Super League
DATE:	15 May 2018
SCORE:	Bristol City Women 0
	Chelsea FC Women 2
VENUE:	Stoke Gifford Stadium
ATTENDANCE:	1,500

#55

Brilliant Blues
League & Cup Double

Hayes' side, who had beaten Arsenal in the FA Cup just ten days earlier, went through the whole season unbeaten and reached the semi-finals of the Champions League.

The atmosphere at the tiny Stoke Gifford Stadium, Bristol, was a far cry from Wembley Stadium, where Chelsea had beaten Arsenal 3-1 in front of 40,000 raucous fans, but managed by assistant Paul Green, the Blues were rarely troubled by the Vixens.

Chelsea took the lead after ten minutes, when Drew Spence headed in a lofted cross from Ji So-yun. Most of the match was played in the City end, with keeper Hedvig Lindahl only forced into one difficult second-half save. The pressure eventually paid off in the 88th minute when Fran Kirby beat her full-back on the right-hand side to send in a low cross for Jonna Anderson to fire into the roof of the net.

After the final whistle, Hayes tweeted: "Get in. A pleasure to watch that from home. Champions of England, we know who we are."

JI SO-YUN & EMMA HAYES

FIXTURE:	FA Cup final
DATE:	19 May 2018
SCORE:	Chelsea 1 Manchester United 0
VENUE:	Wembley Stadium
ATTENDANCE:	87,647

#56

Blues Beat Jose At Wembley

A first-half Eden Hazard penalty was all that was needed for Chelsea to beat Manchester United, managed by former Blues boss Jose Mourinho.

GARY CAHILL
LIFTS THE FA CUP

The match, which turned out to be his last at Chelsea for manager Antonio Conte, reflected his trademark ability to hang on to a lead with resilience and organisation.

Match-winner Hazard had earned his own penalty with a twisting dribble past Phil Jones, drawing a clumsy foul in the area after 22 minutes. He calmly dispatched the spot-kick low to the right of United keeper David de Gea. United, with striker Romelu Lukaku only fit enough to be on the bench, upped the tempo in the second half and had an Alexis Sanchez goal ruled out for offside by VAR - the first time it had been used in a final.

Man of the Match was N'Golo Kante, a tireless defensive buffer who along with 'keeper Thibaut Courtois kept United at bay for Chelsea to win the FA Cup for the eighth time.

EDEN HAZARD

Tributes to Chelsea legend
Ray Wilkins, who also played for Manchester United,
adorned the hoardings and screens in the stadium
following his death from a heart attack
on 4 April 2018, aged 61.

Maurizio Sarri won his only major trophy as Chelsea manager when his team thrashed Arsenal 4-1 in the Europa League final in Baku.

EDEN HAZARD CELEBRATES WITH JORGINHO AFTER SCORING THE THIRD GOAL

FIXTURE: UEFA Europa League final

DATE: 29 May 2019

SCORE: Chelsea 4
Arsenal 1

VENUE: Olympic Stadium

ATTENDANCE: 51,370

#57

Eden Brace Helps Blues Lift Cup

While it turned out be Sarri's last match as manager, it was also the last game in a Blues shirt for Man of the Match Eden Hazard, who scored twice during the game before joining Real Madrid in the summer.

The first half of this London derby with a difference was a dour affair, but came to life shortly after the restart, Olivier Giroud breaking the deadlock against his old club with a deft, low glancing header from an Emerson Palmieri cross.

Pedro added a second ten minutes later, sweeping a Hazard cross into the far corner. Hazard himself coolly scored from the penalty spot, sending his old teammate Petr Cech the wrong way, after Giroud was bundled over in the area by Ainsley Maitland-Niles. The Gunners did pull a goal back with a powerful volley by Alex Iwobi, but minutes later, Hazard gave the Blues a memorable farewell gift when he played a one-two with Giroud and side-footed his second home.

Cech announced his retirement after the match, but he was soon back at the club where he had made 494 senior appearances, as part of the Chelsea coaching staff.

CESAR AZPILICUETA LIFTS THE EUROPA LEAGUE TROPHY

FIXTURE:	UEFA Women's Champions League semi-final, second leg
DATE:	2 May 2021
SCORE:	Chelsea FC Women 4 FC Bayern Munich Ladies 1
VENUE:	Kingsmeadow
ATTENDANCE:	100

#58

Bayern Beaten
To Reach Maiden Final

*Chelsea FC Women overturned a first leg 2-1 loss to beat Bayern Munich
in a thrilling Champions League semi-final, to reach the final for the first time.*

KIRBY CELEBRATES THE FOURTH

The second leg at Kingsmeadow went right down to the wire, with Chelsea defending desperately in the final few minutes before Fran Kirby raced clear in the dying seconds to slot the ball into an empty net for the fourth.

It was Kirby who had put the Blues ahead inside ten minutes with a typically composed finish following a neat one-two with Sam Kerr, before Sarah Zadrazil put Bayern back in the driving seat in the 29th minute with a world-class strike from outside the box, which crashed in off the underside of the bar. Ji So-yun wrested back control two minutes before the break, thumping home the rebound from her own free-kick.

A brilliant glancing header from Pernille Harder looked to have won the tie, but Chelsea still had to survive a late onslaught, with keeper Ann-Katrin Berger making a fine save and captain Magdalena Eriksson clearing off the line.

*The final was disappointing
with the Blues Women soundly beaten 4-0
by Barcelona in Sweden, but the cup run had shown
that the Chelsea team was capable of playing alongside
the very best sides in Europe.*

New Manager Thomas Tuchel, back in the Champions League final for the second year running having been in charge of Paris Saint-Germain when they lost to Bayern Munich, fielded a full strength side with N'Golo Kante back from injury to put in a Man of the Match performance.

JUBILANT SCENES AS CESAR AZPILICUETA LIFTS THE CHAMPIONS LEAGUE TROPHY

FIXTURE: UEFA Champions League final

DATE: 29 May 2021

SCORE: Chelsea 1
Manchester City 0

VENUE: Estadio do Dragao

ATTENDANCE: 14,110

#59

Champions Of Europe, Again!

Playing in their third Champions League final, the first since their away win over Bayern Munich in 2012, Chelsea were triumphant over newly-crowned Premier League champions Manchester City.

Chelsea were forced to make a 39th-minute change when veteran defender Thiago Silva was injured and replaced by Andreas Christensen. But just before half-time, Chelsea took the lead when a through-ball from Mason Mount was controlled by Kai Havertz who went one-on-one with City keeper Ederson before rounding him and passing the ball into an empty net.

Despite a late scare when Riyad Mahrez's half-volley went narrowly over the crossbar, Chelsea were in control throughout and deserved to win a pulsating match.

Thomas Tuchel paid tribute to former manager Frank Lampard who had led the side through the group stage of the competition, a gesture which sealed his approval with the fans.

KAI HAVERTZ SCORES

FIXTURE:	UEFA Super Cup final
DATE:	11 August 2021
SCORE:	Chelsea 1
	Villareal 1
	Chelsea won 6-5
	on penalties
VENUE:	Windsor Park
ATTENDANCE:	10,435

Chelsea Lift Second Super Cup

Champions League winners Chelsea clinched the Super Cup 6-5 on penalties after a 1-1 draw with Spanish club Villareal, winners of the Europa League 2021.

KEPA'S MATCH-WINNING SAVE FROM RAUL ALBIOL

The Blues opened the scoring in the 27th minute when Kai Havertz's low cross from the left was swept home by Hakim Ziyech. In first-half injury-time Villareal almost levelled, Alberto Moreno's superb volley crashing against the underside of the bar, but not crossing the line.

Villareal did equalise though, in the 73rd minute when Man of the Match Gerard Moreno scored with a clinical right-foot finish into the top left-hand corner of the net. With the teams level towards the end of extra-time, Thomas Tuchel replaced keeper Edouard Mendy with Kepa Arrizabalaga, who had a better record of saving penalties in training.

His hunch proved correct. Kepa saved two spot-kicks, the last from veteran Spanish international defender Raul Albiol, who had to score in the sudden death shoot-out to keep the tie alive.

The club's second Super Cup final triumph became even sweeter the next day when it was announced that one of the most prolific strikers in European football, Romelu Lukaku, was returning to the club he supported as a young boy and for whom he had played 15 games in three seasons between 2011 and 2014.

Blue Is The Colour